mango & starblush

poems

Kayleigh Jayshree

In mango & starblush, *Kayleigh Jayshree explores love's raw edges, the mythical, mundane, and mournful. From plush cantos to scathing free verse, Kayleigh balances reflections on past relationships with a delightful, even playful, embrace of the now:* 'Used tissues float like bridal veils'. 'Our bodies are flags pulled through mud'. *This collection is a haunting, beautiful testament to class, love, and the tender violence of connection.*

Malika Booker

'The holes in my vision / must be stars': *Kayleigh Jayshree's debut pamphlet is prismatic, startling, and bold in its formal reach. These are poems alive with dreamy textures and surrealist intimacies. Jayshree maps a landscape that is both textual and visual, a one-of-a-kind locale where relationships, grief, and sensory passions come together in forming a constellation of care. What is offered here is moving and astonishing in equal measure.*

Eric Yip

First published in 2025 by Fourteen Publishing.
fourteenpoems.com

Design and typeset by Stromberg Design.
strombergdesign.co.uk

Proofreading and copy editing by Lara Kavanagh.
lk-copy.com

Printed by P2D Ltd, Westoning, Bedfordshire, UK.

Kayleigh Jayshree has asserted their right to be identified as the author of this work in accordance with the Copyright, Designs and Patents Act 1988.

This book is sold subject to the conditions that it shall not be lent, resold, hired out or otherwise circulated without the publisher's prior consent. Any republishing of the individual works must be agreed in advance.

ISBN: 978-1-0684951-3-7

Contents:

Mango
- in love 10
- Elegy for Dead Chihuahua 11
- The Moth Poem 12
- To Be Beautiful 13
- Orange 14
- Found 15
- Middle Class Moon 16
- by morning 17
- Hyperfixation 18
- Ex-Dream 19
- Jam 20

Starblush
- On Being Ghosted by a Famous Musician 24
- Polar 25
- Footnote 26
- Red-Dream 27
- Duty of Care 28
- THE LOVE OF MY LIFE IS A HAUNTED HOUSE WITH A PICKET FENCE 30
- Room 13 31
- Worm 32
- DNA 33
- Anniversary-Dream 34
- return 35
- Acknowledgements 36

For Sam

Mango

'Things are changing; things are starting to spin, snap, fly off into the blue sleeve of the long afternoon.'

– Mary Oliver, "Last Days"

'the earth's gold breath falling softly / on the dark wood dresser, blue ceramic bowls, / picture frames on the wall. It wafts up / from canyons, carried on the wind, / on the wings of birds, in the rough fur of animals / as they rise from the ground.'

– Danusha Laméris, "Dust"

in love

you're soft as a ghost   your papers unfold

and form snow   on the ikea shelf

the radiator hums   away   to white waves

through vapour   orange   under evening night

bats   gather   outside   curdle together

we're lost owls   lovers   for the first time

so hold me as i cry   under a blood moon

relief from a splinter   unstuck   after nine years

while you're in the bathroom   i google my ex

and learn   the many synonyms   for loser

i'm so   used   to being   pushed

his name is   a bruise   and smoke

looks like   his nose   but   i've spent

time   learning   to   say   no

i fall   on my own   into   a beginning

Elegy for Dead Chihuahua

after Chen Chen

When I eat KFC – especially corn on the cob – I think about my dead chihuahua. He'd eat it, throw up, then shit on the carpet. I prefer cats now. Why didn't anyone tell me that cats are chihuahuas that don't bark?! I want to be Ace Ventura, genderbending in a flat full of flamboyant animals, who'd bite my landlord to death if he arrived without 24 hours' written notice. I don't wish you were alive, Ozzie. You were obese and you ate all my Jammie Dodgers. You nearly killed the same postman three times and I'm certain they blacklisted our house. We fed you cos we loved you, you died; we fussed the tumour into your belly and let it rot. I'm glad you're dead. I don't get bitten by you anymore. Your love stung, Ozzie. And it stunk. You nearly died in 2016. Mum begged you to come back, pressing your belly. I remember your blocked snuffles and stinky breath. You were a little git. I loved you so much, Ozzie. When I was seven, you barked at me for baked beans. I snuck you chocolate, I didn't know it was bad for you.

The Moth Poem

would-be anniversary

She sees the little lost one everywhere,
eyes on the dead moths by her windowsill.

I see what was: rosy maple moths flower
on her fingertips, a weaver's wave moth

in the countryside the day she broke down
and I wasn't there. Hummingbird moths,

wings a heartbeat. Small, too quick.
On the would-be anniversary

I remember when I couldn't leave my house.
She crocheted gifts for Christmas

gave reminders to drink lemon water
and stroked my hair

when I was broken hearted.
Years later, I still buy moth postcards

trying to mend the hole nobody made
with moth shaped safety pins.

Our friendship stronger than a birthright

vivid as sunset. Through loss our lives
threaded together.

Moth is half *mother,* a scar on her chest
she's had for as long as she can remember.

To Be Beautiful

A self-erasure

```
                        you
stopped   trying    years ago    the                         sound
rattles   your      voice        warped     when      you    hid
freckled  teeth                                              your
eyes      are       bald         from       pulling   out    lashes
learned   to                                                 shield
yourself  from      men          keep                        falling
for       bullies                they                        won't
let       you                    love                        them
still     envy                   flashes    like             diver's
bells                 you        wanted     to               be
a         siren                  you're     a                lighthouse
creaking  over                   storms     helping          people
who                 don't        see        you              cover
that      body                   from       thick            hands
pink                as                                       shame
you're              a   skinny   little     meal             licked
bone      clean         and      desperate  you              fell
in                                                           love
with      the       first        person     you              met
his       fingers   stiff    and                             unforgiving
as        sandpaper for                     six              years
you                 are                     in               bed
                    waiting
```

Orange

forced to eat the fruit
when i was too young

now we unpeel together
and trust textures in bits

threaded pith and rough skin
i swallow the inside fully

a pillow's down   a wet print
a curled underlip

Found

He parts the stars into waves, pearls through darkest fog
a half formed half woman beats her claws on sand walls, blue thread

winds through the labyrinth. Seasalt on his forearms, her sweat meets
his tracks on the ground. She chokes on his thread, this story is ours

clipped galaxies in your coiled hair. The holes in my vision
must be stars, dead before knowing what was found there.

Middle Class Moon

I clutch a shampoo bottle
in my friend's circular bath.
This room is large enough

to have its own system of time.
Circlets of noise swallow the days.
I slide my head under:

Gunk from a former life evaporates in star anise
and sandalwood. The water is a gown
and I am on stage accepting an award.

There are family members to thank. A rapt audience:
applauding bubbles, a crushed crowd of soap
dispensers and shampoo bottles. I would not be

here without you all. I grab her non-slip mat
the plastic folds deep as craters. Orbiting the middle class
moon, this is the bath, cold and planetary.

It could be Monday. I don't rush
floating in a sensory deprivation tank, deprived
of ever feeling deprived of anything.

I step out swaddled in organic cotton
the tattoos on my legs are scribbled reminders –
marks in a passport, an origin I can't wash off.

by morning

bruised feet
press
on

the
bedframe
he

rubs
suncream
on

my
ankles
the

icing
sugar
texture

wets
my
furry legs

spreads
through
tattoos

winding
a
spiral

unused

to
stillness
slick

as
jellied
eels

white
salted
slugs

my
turgid
body

relaxes

his
hair
curls

our
blur
each

blink
a small
moon

caught

Hyperfixation

Wikipedia: you downloaded the app, satisfied inane and inconsequential curiosities, side by side searching: *when did Nixon die? eHarmony, Justin Hartley, Gnarls Barkley, Channel 5, Disambiguation (Disambiguation)*. You notice my sweet tooth and we gorge on white chocolate rings from M&S, plastic snakeskin packaging strewed across the floor. Figs sliced by serrated spoons, bananas cut into semi circles, broken in half by drummer's thumbs. Kissing outside the hedgehog crossing, then fastening a hedgehog pin badge to your work lanyard. I haven't been afraid since we met. I never thought of safety in the long term. Past men come back in snatches, blocked messages, scraped up plaque, sand stuck in old socks. Knowing I should have always been happy sometimes makes it worse. For all the time I lost hoping awful people would be better. I'm coming back from a party, shivering from the snow and you're halfway through a five-hour M&M advert compilation, mouthing along, nearly asleep, dropping your phone in your face in odd intervals, then you wake up, smile at me.

Ex-Dream

if we swing wildly it's flight when we run
to each other it's punches when we looked
at the graves we saw our lives
in other people's names as the afternoon traced
your grandmother's house we were ugly
before we knew each other we built something gentle
to leave i don't know if it's New Years Eve
or a half-empty social house where you smell like
lavender or mango you fall asleep on my arm
or shoulder or hers used tissues float
like bridal veils and it's so hard to talk
i broke my nose in a dream bled
in the morning loss entered us before we knew
fed us until we starved lit up
our starcrossed bodies we became
who we were before we were born
someday you'll come back you'll finally
find a song for me turn and sing
and you turn not finding me as i'm waiting
where your voice wouldn't reach

Jam

gentle tufts pulled
rough at the stem

unwind
in my left palm

hands swing
into bell petals

velvet
afternoon air
butters the sunset

in snatches
the sky creased

over rain blue
dusted glass

a cowbell rings low
past lives ripen and echo.

Starblush

'As a species / we dreamed. We used to / dream.'
– Jorie Graham, "Belief System"

'I eat the stars. / Those nights, lying on my back / I suck them from the quenching dark / Til they are all, all inside me / Pepper hot and sharp.'
– Rebecca Elson, "Antidotes to Fear of Death"

On Being Ghosted by a Famous Musician

Nobody knew he had a glass eye, but when we were alone he'd pop it in and out, like a cuckoo clock, as a sort of intimate party trick. I was surprised by how real it looked, how it followed you around the room, interrupted only by blinks. I always wanted to touch it, but he never let me. He stopped talking to me because of that. But I didn't mind it. What put me off him was his hangnails, flicking them from his fingers. Pulling them out with his teeth, never bothered by the blood.

(REPRISE)

When I listen to his music, I imagine an empty swimming pool and a pink diving board with yellow polka dots that look a bit like patches of vomit. I see an orchestra playing his songs in the space where water should rest. I climb the ladder and prepare to dive. At the very least I'll break my neck, but something about his music makes me want to hit the bottom.

Polar

after "Scheherazade" by Richard Siken

What about bipolar, mania, those pearly scars. Was it gorgeous?

I weighed the future in a clenched razor.
There was no success, I dug my own grave. Went crazy.
Didn't die, did it again.

Readers have time for visible collarbones
and ageless coloured comets. They want
to throw pennies, lick salt-ridden stories, smell blood.

*I say, nobody wants to see artists get old. When you're honest
people get bored.*
Pain is ugly:

Wetting myself on a paper mattress
the days scratched out, shared lipstick with criminals
minds kissed by madness.

*Tell me how pain is forever, tell me we'll get used to it, she says.
Please tell me you die at the end.*
Our bodies are flags pulled through mud.

Footnote

A Wiki-poem

orbiting dark matter[1] liquid seeds
are[2] systems[3] that ripple deepen[4]
break or form[5] divide or co-exist[6]
in volcanic boundaries[7] the brightness
of a star[8] is distinct from twilight[9]
that cloud-coloured sky[10] in the age[11]
of the river valley[12] ultramarine specks[13]
are swam in by wild ancestors [14] painted
red[15] on war horses in heavy cavalry[16]
our punched pattern[17]: disease [18] a network
of threads[19] rose-coloured spots[20] test tunnels
below the ground[21] growing in bone marrow[22]
your evil twin[23] cannot help[24] your evil twin[25]
is on the right side of history[26]

1   https://en.wikipedia.org/wiki/Galaxy
2   https://en.wikipedia.org/wiki/Chocolate
3   https://en.wikipedia.org/wiki/Gardening
4   https://en.wikipedia.org/wiki/Loneliness
5   https://en.wikipedia.org/wiki/Pangaea
6   https://en.wikipedia.org/wiki/Interpersonal_relationship
7   https://en.wikipedia.org/wiki/Tectonic_Plates_(film)
8   https://en.wikipedia.org/wiki/Star
9   https://en.wikipedia.org/wiki/Sunset
10 https://en.wikipedia.org/wiki/Grey
11 https://en.wikipedia.org/wiki/Cosmic_Inflation
12 https://en.wikipedia.org/wiki/Watercolour_Painting
13 https://en.wikipedia.org/wiki/Illuminated_manuscript#Engrossing:_The_process_of_illumination
14 https://en.wikipedia.org/wiki/Tomato
15 https://en.wikipedia.org/wiki/Clown
16 https://en.wikipedia.org/wiki/Equestrianism
17 https://en.wikipedia.org/wiki/Pink
18 https://en.wikipedia.org/wiki/Disease
19 https://en.wikipedia.org/wiki/Fungus#Morphology
20 https://en.wikipedia.org/wiki/Typhoid_fever
21 https://en.wikipedia.org/wiki/Typhoid_fever
22 https://en.wikipedia.org/wiki/Typhoid_fever
23 https://en.wikipedia.org/wiki/Ego_death
24 https://en.wikipedia.org/wiki/Catchphrase#History
25 https://en.wikipedia.org/wiki/Ego_death
26 https://en.wikipedia.org/wiki/The_Right_Side_of_History

Red-Dream

after Powers of Ten (1977)

lakeside october boats
lie at their docks
as people carry boxes
of wine to the park
a tilted planet follows
fringed stars that shake
the evening into view burnt
gold scatters into the sky
dizzy clouds surround us
faint and vanish the red edge
borders the field where we saw
galaxies together

Duty of Care

nuts
again
bolting
in
white
gripp-
ed
socks
sliding
on
floors
baby,
im
sparkling
mad
storms
in
the
floorboards
outside
stands
the
ward
doctor
with
keys
to
my
room
turning
havent
died
in
days
too
old
for
angst
but
im
thin
-ner
than
ever
a
wasp
in
my
womb
plastic
plates
thrown

fireproof
doors
melting
snow
smashed
baubles
from
half
hopeful
christmas
trees
i
was
meant
to
be
something
as
a
girl
i
shaved
with
dad's
razor
blood
fizzes
like
cola
we
can't
go
in
the
garden
i
cant
swim
i
was
supposed
to
be
some
thing
help
the
shower
is
flooding

THE LOVE OF MY LIFE IS A HAUNTED HOUSE WITH A PICKET FENCE

after Phoebe Bridgers

Squirrels scuttle across the front garden into an unmowed island. Her paint is chipped, a freckled fence. She's a creaking window, all encompassing. The ghosts flutter around the house and I realise things are haunted for a reason. I'll become a madwoman in her attic. She shudders with the wind like an old sailboat, and I build her steady, build her clean.

Room 13

There is a man outside my hospital door
his knuckled knock is a skeleton key.

My pyjamas hang like a circus tent. One foot
drenched from walks I made when asleep.

I'm tended to like stitching in a wound:
Sewn shut. Dissolved in water.

Worm
after Chen Chen

The San Pellegrino on my relative's coffee table is telling me to *do more of what I am capable of*. The aluminium has a tooth-like glint. I'm in my overdraft, sleeping in North London. *I'm not even capable of buying a sandwich* I want to say back, but the can keeps fizzing, interrupting. A news reporter on the TV is waxing on and on about private schools and I can't help but think about the biology teacher who lost my coursework and got sacked for texting a Year 7. I am trying to be more patient with rich people. It's part of my work-expensed anger management class. There's a beagle outside yelping at me. Can't you see I'm busy? I'm trying to be alone. His floppy ears remind me of an ex-boyfriend. The astroturf outside looks like it stinks, the beagle is doing tricks to impress me. Flatscreen plays adverts of gambling sites and I feel like an evil little worm. I wish someone would crush me. A wasp is hovering on the can now. My relative told me her children's school fees are more than I earn in a year. Why can't I stop needing money? Please tread on me so I can die. Flatscreen moans about Corbyn and I've decided to insist on a supremely rich version of myself, who rolls and unrolls the same cigarette, who always wears stained clothes, who knows Spanish but never uses it, and has a car that goes everywhere, forever. I'm trying to be brilliant but I have run out of money.

DNA

Hospital   car

    park: close

with   death

      a ringing alarm
no laces   no razors

   discharge   papers

moth wings   pressed

      white lined
  notebooks   sick buckets

murmur   into

   gossamer   grey hair

      dust

  plucked   in this

     place
where

 i
   become
      old

for the first time.

Anniversary-Dream

Clouds are flowering over
sea caves made of salt
and gold. The stars have wings
like everything else.
A marriage unimagined
close as we'd ever got.
We are all afraid
you say. Loving
what is easy;
three white butterflies
starved flags of surrender.

return

they
churn
in unison

slow
lengths
of white

jawless
fish
under ice

wait
for
earth

Acknowledgements

Thank you to the teams at *Butcher's Dog, fourteen poems, Young Poets Network,* and *Ink Sweat & Tears* for publishing several of these poems. Thank you to Ben, Lara, and Janine at fourteen poems for your hard work and your support on this pamphlet.

A special thank you to Tim and Orysia Sutton. Thank you to Steve Dearden, Francesca Haig, Malika Booker, and The Writing Squad, without whose support this work would not exist. Thank you to Rory Waterman, Roma Havers, Rory Thorp, and Jay Mitra, whose editorial feedback has consistently improved my writing. Thank you to Chloe Elliott whose poetry has inspired the '-dream' poems in this pamphlet. Thanks to Ashleigh Pritchard, who read the first poem I wrote over ten years ago and has encouraged me ever since. And thank you to my nan, Catherine Hicks, who also writes poems and has supported me more than she'll ever know. Thank you to Alle Bloom and Phill Varin.

The sources of 'Anniversary-Dream' are as follows, in order of appearance:

Sylvia Plath "The Moon and the Yew Tree" in *Ariel, The Restored Edition*

Nina Mingya Powles "Last summer we were underwater" in *Magnolia 木蘭*

Nina Mingya Powles "'Love letter in lotus leaves" in *Magnolia 木蘭*

Rebecca Elson "Aberration" in *A Responsibility to Awe*

Lucy Mercer "Mirror" in *Emblem*

Rebecca Goss "There was a swing" in *Latch*

Karen McCarthy Woolf "The Calf" in *An Aviary of Small Birds*

Rebecca Goss "Hounds" in *Latch*

Rachel Long "Hotel Art, Barcelona" in *My Darling from the Lions*

Mary Oliver "Starfish" in *New and Selected Poems: Volume One*

Karen McCarthy Woolf "White Butterflies" in *An Aviary of Small Birds*

Fiona Benson "Ace of Bass" in *Vertigo & Ghost*

Rebecca Elson "Hanging out his Boxer Shorts to Dry" in *A Responsibility to Awe*